ENCOUNTER

Come to Know Him

LYNDA LEE KJARTANSON

Tellwell Talent
www.tellwell.ca

ISBN
978-1-77302-538-4 (Hardcover)
978-1-77302-539-1 (Paperback)
978-1-77302-537-7 (eBook)

Table of Contents

ACKNOWLEDGMENTS

I acknowledge the Lord,
God the Father, Son and Holy Spirit
that He will direct me.

Trust in the Lord with all your heart
And do not lean on your own understanding.
In all your ways acknowledge Him,
And He will make your paths straight.
(Proverbs 3:5-7)

THANK YOU!

Father, I thank You for loving me and rescuing me. I thank You for meeting with me and the gifts You have shared with me.

I would like to thank the many people who have been there for me during my journey. Psalm 118:7 says that *"He is among those who help me."* Thank you so very much for the help I have received along the way.

Give thanks. I give thanks for what the Lord has done in my life. Where I have been broken, I have been made whole. May what I have gained through my experiences be multiplied to those who receive and may they also be filled with the Bread of Life and Living Water: our Lord Jesus, Yeshua the Messiah.

PREFACE

During my quiet times with the Lord, I hear from Him in different ways. I may get a single word, which I will then look up in the dictionary and find references for in the Bible. At other times I will hear a word or a phrase, and then—as I write it down—more words will flow, coming as poetry. Sometimes I will hear a scripture reference or be directed to a specific location in the Bible to read. I began to see that there were themes emerging. I have grouped them together here to express the fellowship I have with the Father, his Son, Jesus Christ, and the Holy Spirit, to encourage you to encounter Him.

> "... so that you too, may have fellowship with us; and
> indeed our fellowship is with the Father, and with His
> Son Jesus Christ." (1 John 1:3)

As the Prophet Jeremiah says, "The Word of the Lord that came to me," I would like to convey the words that have come to me, with the hope of encouraging you to know the Living God. I write these things that your joy may be made full.

INTRODUCTION

I want to introduce you to a really good friend of mine, Jesus or *Yeshua*, the Messiah and The Holy Spirit.

Through my journey, I have encountered the Presence of God and have come to know Him. I first met him as Jesus, but have come to know Him as *Yeshua*, the Messiah.

There were turning points in my life where I went from knowing about God to knowing Him. He says that when you search for Him with all your heart, you will find Him. I hadn't always put my whole heart into seeking God. It takes a decision and effort to grow a relationship with Him, like any other relationship. There are different ways of communicating and getting to know each other. One of these is sitting still and listening for His Voice.

One of my first encounters with God was at summer camp. The camp counsellor had us go find a quiet place and wait until we heard from God. Well, I may not remember now exactly what I heard Him say, but I do know that I came away from that experience knowing that He was real. The camp counsellor had me say a prayer with her asking Jesus into my heart. I experienced a definite change from this point forward. I earnestly read the copy of *The* Good News Bible that she had given me for the remainder of that summer. I did not keep up my relationship with Him, however.

Many years later, I had an encounter with God and met the Holy Spirit. This truly was a life-changing experience and there would be no turning back. I have come to know the Holy Spirit through the various means that he speaks to me: the still small voice, His Word, journaling, prayer, worship, pictures, dreams. I will get a word from Him, which I then look up the meaning of, expanding upon the message.

I am including poetry that I received through times of intimacy with the Holy Spirit. As I shared my heart with Him, He shared with me. When I have read these poems to others, they were blessed by them. I hope that you will be, too.

Come and meet with Him.

Come and experience His Presence.

Come and really get to know Him.

Come to Me...

Come follow Me...

Be still and know that I am God.

He invites you to come to Him.

May you have a real life-changing encounter with God!

CHAPTER I

ENCOUNTER

Come and Meet Him

Encounter:

To meet
To come upon face-to-face
To come upon or experience
A particular kind of meeting or experience with another person
(Definition from www.merriam-webster.com)

Come and meet Him face-to-face. Moses asked God for such an encounter. You can have this face-to-face encounter with the Living God. It is something that happens on the inside. God does not judge by the outward appearance, but by what is in our hearts, our minds, thoughts and feelings. May you have an experience of encountering the love of God. Draw near with your heart. Seek Him and you will find Him. An encounter is to experientially know Him.

How do we meet Him?

In the Bible, the written Word of God, you will meet Him.

"In the beginning was the Word. The Word was with God, and the Word was God." (John 1:1)

"But whoever did receive Him, those trusting in His name, to these He gave the right to become children of God." (John 1:12)

"By this the love of God was manifested in us, that God has sent His only begotten Son into the world so that we might live through Him. In this is love, not that we loved God, but that He loved us and sent His Son to be the propitiation for our sins.

Whoever confesses that Jesus is the Son of God, God abides in him, and he in God. We have come to know and have believed the love which God has for us. God is love, and the one who abides in love abides in God, and God abides in him." (1 John 4:9, 10, 15, 16)

"But what does it say? "The word is near you, in your mouth and in your heart"—that is, the word of faith which we are preaching, that if you confess with your mouth Jesus as Lord, and believe in your heart that God raised Him from the dead, you will be saved; for with the heart a person believes, resulting in righteousness, and with the mouth he confesses, resulting in salvation."

"'Whoever will call on the name of the Lord will be saved.'" (Romans 10:8-10 & 13)

This is where my life changed, when I called on Jesus. I became more aware of how He wanted me to live. It has been a journey of progress, changing from who I was. I have learned more of the Word of God and I have grown to know Him more. It is an adventure. I am enjoying the encounters I am having along the way.

He loves you so much that He sent His only Son to make a way back into a relationship with the Heavenly Father. When you have had an encounter with the Love of God, there is nothing that can separate you from it. We have tried everything and yet come up empty. Nothing else here on earth can make you as full or joyful. This is a love that fills every gap, every question, every need and the longing of your heart. Come experience His Love.

I have had encounters that caused me to know the reality and the love of Christ. I experienced an overwhelming sense of love, acceptance and warmth, giving me such a profound sense of well-being. He cares about us so much that even little details and concerns matter. One time, I had the thought of wanting a chocolate bar, during a difficult time. There was someone who felt to call, come to visit and bring me a chocolate bar. I was very touched by this kindness. He cares! The little things matter.

When you have had the experience of knowing His Love, there is a peace and well-being that occurs. It is a peace that we can't explain, because it is the very Presence of God and not anything of our own human understanding. May you come to experientially *encounter* this peace and love.

During times of being in God's Presence, I would hear words from the Lord that inspired me to write poetry. Below is a poem on the power and cost of His Love for us.

POWER OF LOVE

Jesus, Jesus, Jesus!

Oh what power the force of Love
Come to rescue us by death on a cross
Oh what Love
Oh what Cost
How the Love and the pain mingled and
mixed in the chambers of His heart
Hear the Cry,
"How much more must I bear?
Oh Abba, Abba"
And then there, the breaking point.
To others it looks like death and gloom
But on the inside the Light of Heaven looms.
No more darkness
No more gloom
As Love enters your heart
And heals the hurt and wounds.
For He came to heal the broken-hearted and make them whole.
Holy that is.
Consecrated
Set apart
Righteous by His Blood He shed
Washing
Healing
Heaven revealing
Let Love enter your heart.
Jesus, Jesus, Jesus.

All who call upon His Name shall be saved.

You were bought with the highest price of His only Son, so that He could have a personal relationship with you, His creation. When we call out His Name, "Jesus" or "Yeshua," we will be saved.

Jesus, I call on Your Name and ask You to fill my heart. Thank you!

CHAPTER 2

COME

Come to Him

Come:

Move toward the speaker or the place where he is or will be; approach: come this way
Arrive
Appear; light comes and goes.
Reach; extend
Happen; take place; occur
Be caused; result
Be born; get to be; turn out to be; become
Be brought; pass; enter
Occur in the mind; the solution of the problem has come to me.
Come back: return
(Definition from Canadian Intermediate Dictionary 1979 edition
and www.merriam-webster.com)

> *"Come to Me, all who are weary and heavy-laden, and*
> *I will give you rest. Take My yoke upon you and learn*
> *from Me, for I am gentle and humble in heart, and you*
> *will find rest for your souls. For My yoke is easy and My*
> *burden is light."* (Matthew 11:28-30)

*"Jesus said to him, 'I am the way, and the truth, and the
life; no one comes to the Father but through Me.'"* (John
14:6)

*"Then Jesus spoke to them again, saying, 'I am the light of
the world. He who follows Me shall not walk in darkness,
but have the light of life.'"* (John 8:12)

I observed that in the word "encounter," there is a *u* in the middle.
It is up to *"us"*, to you (*u*) to decide. Will you turn to Him or away
from Him? While travelling in Israel, I saw a very unique occur-
rence. On the side of the road, there was a road sign with a tree
growing in the post. I felt I needed to take a picture of it to show
us symbolically living in Christ.

We are to move toward Him, to approach Him, to reach for Him
and go His way and arrive. When you come to Him, you will be
born again and made new. You will have His Spirit in you. It is by

this spirit that you will be given direction, knowledge and wisdom. He will bring you through situations and give you solutions to problems. Maybe you once knew Him and turned away. Come back. Return to Him.

JOURNEY INTO ETERNITY

For upon this new journey
You will embark,
To travel to your future,
A new world to see,
New ways of doing things,
A new way to be
Set apart in Me
Think like Me
Act like Me
Look like Me

Do not be discouraged,
Nor dismayed.
Come away with Me,
The King of Kings,
The Lord of Lords.
With My Spirit,
I will lead you
Into all Truth;
Provide you the grace and strength,
To go through.
Go through all uncertainty.
For My way is a sure way,
An endless way.
Follow Me into Eternity!

Love Your Father,
Abba God

"And this is life eternal, that they might know thee the only true God, and Jesus Christ, whom thou hast sent." (John 17:3)

"My sheep hear My voice, and I know them, and they follow Me." (John 10:27)

CHAPTER 3

KNOW

Come to Know Him

"He says, "Be still, and know that I am God; I will be exalted among the nations, I will be exalted in the earth." (Psalm 46:10, NIV)

"Know that the Lord Himself is God; It is He who has made us, and not we ourselves; We are His people and the sheep of His pasture." (Psalm 100:3)

Know:

Be sure of; have true information
Have firmly in the mind or memory
Be aware of
Be sure or certain because of experience or knowledge
Be acquainted with; be familiar with
(Definition from Canadian Intermediate Dictionary 1979 edition)

Yada:

To know
Learn to know
To perceive and see, find out and discern

To know by experience
To recognise, admit, acknowledge, and confess
To consider
To know, be acquainted with
To be made known, be or become known, be revealed
To make oneself known
(Definition from *Strong's H3045*)

To be sure that we have the right information, let us look to the source, the truth, the Word of God. As we read the Word and meditate on it, we become acquainted with Him. The more time we spend reading the Bible, the better we get to know Him. Reading it out loud and meditating on it will firmly plant the Word in our minds and hearts. Consider the people you know best. They are the people you have spent the most time with. You may even know what they are thinking or how they will do things a certain way. This is the relationship God wants to have with you. The more you read His Word, the more He will reveal Himself to you. You will become more familiar with how He talks to you. He will speak to you about certain situations through His Word. He wants to make himself known to you.

To know Him is to love Him. Love Him with all your heart, mind, thoughts and feelings. Place him first in your thoughts, giving Him priority in your attention and affections. Seek Him as for hidden riches. He is a treasure to be found. We love Him because He first loved us.

In Deuteronomy 6:3-7 He gave us commandment to Love Him with all our heart, soul and might.

> "*One of the scribes came and heard them arguing, and recognizing that He had answered them well, asked Him, 'What commandment is the foremost of all?' Jesus answered, 'The foremost is, 'HEAR, O ISRAEL! THE LORD OUR GOD IS ONE LORD; AND YOU SHALL LOVE THE LORD YOUR GOD WITH ALL YOUR HEART, AND*

WITH ALL YOUR SOUL, AND WITH ALL YOUR MIND,
AND WITH ALL YOUR STRENGTH. THE SECOND IS THIS,
'YOU SHALL LOVE YOUR NEIGHBOR AS YOURSELF."
There is no other commandment greater than these.'"
(Mark 12:28-31)

One of the verses that most strongly impacted me is Matthew 7:23, which says, "I never knew you".

> *"Not everyone who says to Me, 'Lord, Lord,' shall enter*
> *the kingdom of heaven, but he who does the will of My*
> *Father in heaven. Many will say to Me in that day, 'Lord,*
> *Lord, have we not prophesied in Your name, cast out*
> *demons in Your name, and done many wonders in Your*
> *name?' And then I will declare to them, 'I never knew*
> *you; depart from Me, you who practice lawlessness!'"*
> (Matthew 7:21-23 NKJV)

I Want to Know Him!

When I read this, I had a "God moment": one of those moments when you know that a Truth has penetrated and become real. I want to KNOW God and be part of His Kingdom. I want to cultivate and grow an intimate relationship with the Lord. I don't want something that is only surface or phony. I want to really *know* Him and to love him with all my heart.

So, how do we know Him?

We get to know him by spending time with him. It is a matter of the heart—putting him first. Once we have opened the door and invited Him in, he is there with us at all times. We can acknowledge him wherever we are and in whatever we are doing.

But not by my words, but by His Words:

"Behold, I stand at the door and knock; if anyone hears My voice and opens the door, I will come in to him and will dine with him, and he with Me." (Revelation 3:20)

"So Jesus said to them again, 'Truly, truly, I say to you, I am the door of the sheep. All who came before Me are thieves and robbers, but the sheep did not hear them. I am the door; if anyone enters through Me, he will be saved, and will go in and out and find pasture."

" I am the good shepherd, and I know My own and My own know Me, even as the Father knows Me and I know the Father; and I lay down My life for the sheep. I have other sheep, which are not of this fold; I must bring them also, and they will hear My voice; and they will become one flock with one shepherd." (John 10:7-9, 14-16)

"Beloved, do not believe every spirit, but test the spirits to see whether they are from God, because many false prophets have gone out into the world. By this you know the Spirit of God: every spirit that confesses that Jesus Christ has come in the flesh is from God; and every spirit that does not confess Jesus is not from God; this is the spirit of the antichrist, of which you have heard that it is coming, and now it is already in the world. You are from God, little children, and have overcome them; because greater is He who is in you than he who is in the world.

God Is Love

Beloved, let us love one another, for love is from God; and everyone who loves is born of God and knows God.

By this we know that we abide in Him and He in us, because He has given us of His Spirit.

Whoever confesses that Jesus is the Son of God, God abides in him, and he in God. We have come to know and have believed the love which God has for us. God is love, and the one who abides in love abides in God, and God abides in him." (1 John 4:1-4, 7,13,15,16)

Jesus, the Word of God:

I come to you. I want to know you, to perceive and experience Your Presence and Love. Help me to learn more about you. I admit and confess that I have been far from you and sinned. I receive your forgiveness. I ask you to come abide inside me and reveal who you are and what you are like.

Thank you!

On February 14, 2014, which is Valentine's Day, I had been spending time with God and reflecting on His Love. I got the word, "ransomed." I then put on some instrumental music and was going to spend some quiet time in God's Presence. As I did, I received the words for this poem:

RANSOMED

Ransomed; He paid the price.
Once for all.

Paid the Price.
His life for mine

He paid the price
His Blood for mine
He paid the price

He answered the CALL
He paid it all
What greater Love than this?
To lay down His life for mine
A greater friend than a brother
Greater Love than any other
He loved me more
And redeemed my soul

O Lord, I answer Your Call
The call above all
Come enter in
You knock on my heart's door
And I let You in

He paid the price
To set me free
The thief & the robber
Must set me free
I have been RANSOMED
I am ransomed and free

I declare Your Glory
You have ransomed me
You came to give me life abundantly
Free indeed
Ransomed by Thee

Oh Lord, how You Love me
Ransomed and free

Abide in me
Ransomed and free

Ransomed and free
Come live in me
Ransomed and free
His Blood shed for me

"For there is one God, and one mediator also between God and men, the man Christ Jesus, who gave Himself as a ransom for all, the testimony given at the proper time." (1 Timothy 2:5, 6)

To those who reverentially fear Him,

To those who seek Him and want to know Him,

He will impart a greater knowing of His heart.

Come and know Me more

Search for Me

Seek Me

You will find Me

CHAPTER 4

PURPOSE

Come Be Like Him

Purpose:

Something one intends to get or do; plan; aim; intention
The object or end for which a thing is made, done, used, etc.
On purpose, with a purpose, not an accident
(Definition from Canadian Intermediate Dictionary 1979 edition)

We have been created for a purpose.

You are not an accident.

God has a great plan for you.

God created us in His Image.

He predestined us to be conformed to the image of Christ.

*"And we know that God causes all things to work together
for good to those who love God, to those who are called
according to His purpose. For those whom He foreknew,*

He also predestined to become conformed to the image of His Son, so that He would be the firstborn among many brethren; and these whom He predestined, He also called; and these whom He called, He also justified; and these whom He justified, He also glorified." (Romans 8:28, 29)

"In Him also we have obtained an inheritance, being pre-destined according to the purpose of Him who works all things according to the counsel of His will." (Ephesians 1:11, NKJV)

We are to be His Reflection.

Reflection:

Reflecting or being reflected
A likeness; image
An effect produced by an influence
Thinking; careful thinking
A thought, idea, or opinion formed or a remark made as a result of meditation
Consideration of some subject matter, idea, or purpose
(Definition from Canadian Intermediate Dictionary 1979 edition)

"But we all, with unveiled face, beholding as in a mirror the glory of the Lord, are being transformed into the same image from glory to glory, just as by the Spirit of the Lord." (2 Corinthians 3:18)

Become like Him.

Reflect on His Image.

Be transformed into His image.

Be Imitators of God.

"*Therefore be imitators of God, as beloved children; and walk in love, just as Christ also loved you.*" (Ephesians 5:1, 2)

"*Therefore I urge you, brethren, by the mercies of God, to present your bodies a living and holy sacrifice, acceptable*

*to God, which is your spiritual service of worship. And
do not be conformed to this world, but be transformed
by the renewing of your mind, so that you may prove
what the will of God is, that which is good and accept-
able and perfect."* (Romans 12:1, 2)

Look into the Word of God and find out how He sees you. Speak
the Word of God out loud to yourself, or even while looking
in a mirror, to renew your mind. Personalize the scripture like
this sample:

I am no longer of this world. I am a new creature in Christ Jesus.
I put off the old man and put on the new man. I have the mind
of Christ and can do all things through Christ who strengthens
me. Greater is He that is in me than he who is in the world. I am
brave, strong and of good courage. I have been given a spirit of
power, love and a sound mind.

*"This Book of the Law shall not depart from your mouth,
but you shall meditate in it day and night, that you may
observe to do according to all that is written in it. For
then you will make your way prosperous, and then you
will have good success."* (Joshua 1:8, NKJV)

*"But his delight is in the law of the Lord, and in His law
he meditates day and night."* (Psalm 1:2)

In Joshua 1:8, to *meditate* is not merely to reflect on something, but
to recite or speak by repetition, much like saying memory verses.

When we reflect on, or meditate on, His Word, saying it out loud
causes it to become part of us, and we reflect him.

*"Therefore be imitators of God, as beloved children;
and walk in love, just as Christ also loved you and gave
Himself up for us, an offering and a sacrifice to God as
a fragrant aroma.*

"But immorality or any impurity or greed must not even be named among you, as is proper among saints; and there must be no filthiness and silly talk, or coarse jesting, which are not fitting, but rather giving of thanks. For this you know with certainty, that no immoral or impure person or covetous man, who is an idolater, has an inheritance in the kingdom of Christ and God.

"Let no one deceive you with empty words, for because of these things the wrath of God comes upon the sons of disobedience. Therefore do not be partakers with them; for you were formerly darkness, but now you are Light in the Lord; walk as children of Light (for the fruit of the Light consists in all goodness and righteousness and truth), trying to learn what is pleasing to the Lord. Do not participate in the unfruitful deeds of darkness, but instead even expose them; for it is disgraceful even to speak of the things which are done by them in secret. But all things become visible when they are exposed by the light, for everything that becomes visible is light." (Ephesians 5:1-13)

Come to Him as Little Children

Little children imitate their parents. They will repeat sounds, becoming more and more familiar with them until they are speaking and understanding a language. Come to the Word of the Father daily, reading it and becoming acquainted with Him. Get to know Him and His family. You are now part of this family. Speak the Word out loud, allowing it to grow in your heart. The Word of God is alive, quick and powerful.

From Philippians 4:8:

"Whatever things are true

Whatever things are noble

Whatever things are just

Whatever things are pure

Whatever things are lovely

Whatever things are of good report, any virtue, anything praiseworthy

Meditate on these things – think on these things only!"

God is good.

God is noble.

God is holy.

God is pure.

God is perfect.

God is just.

God is trustworthy.

God is faithful.

God is true.

God is lovely.

God is good!

Oh so good.

He is good to me!

Meditate on God. Reflect on Him!

HIS PURPOSE

"Everyone who believes that Jesus is the Christ (the Messiah, the Anointed) is born of God [that is, reborn from above—spiritually transformed, renewed, and set apart for His purpose], and everyone who loves the Father also loves the child born of Him." (1 John 5:1, AMP)

"But for this purpose I came to this hour." (John 12:27, NKJV)

"I am the resurrection, and the life: he that believeth in me, though he were dead, yet shall he live." (John 11:25)

CHAPTER 5

ABIDE

Abide in Him

"Do you not know that you are a temple of God and that the Spirit of God dwells in you?" (1 Corinthians 3:16)

THE PROMISE FULFILLED

(Inspired by Mathew 1:23)

The Promise
The Birth,
Here on earth.
Immanuel
God with us
Fulfilled
Yeshua Messiah
Returned
Abiding in us
King of Glory

"Whoever confesses that Jesus is the Son of God, God abides in him, and he in God." (1 John 4:15)

Abide:

Stay; remain
Dwell; continue to live in
Stand firm
Wait for
Abide by
Accept and follow out
Remain faithful to; fulfill
(Definition from Canadian Intermediate Dictionary 1979 edition)

I think there is a real mystery to Jesus abiding in us and in our abiding in God's Presence, where the two become one. It is the very reality of the Living God dwelling on the inside of us. We do not need to go searching the world to find him. He has come down to earth to dwell in each of us. As we sit still and wait upon Him, we will have personal encounters with him.

Part of abiding with Him is preparing. In our homes we organize and decorate to make a place to feel like home. We can prepare the atmosphere for times of hearing from God by playing worship music or peaceful music with scripture. I am sure, like me, you also like to receive something new. We need to make room for the new by getting rid of old things. Ask the Holy Spirit to direct you to remove things that hinder your new life. It may be decluttering the home in which you live. Maybe there are items that do not glorify God or have some attachment to the old life. Clear away the distractions so that you will be able to focus fully on Jesus.

We cultivate a relationship with Him through various means of expressing our worship, love and adoration of Him. We were each created with unique personalities, talents and gifts; therefore, we will have individual ways of expressing ourselves. Take time to spend with Him. Go for a walk and talk with Jesus. Find a quiet place and be still before Him, waiting quietly but expectantly to hear from him. Journaling is another way of communicating with the Father. Focus on Jesus, write out your thoughts and questions. Then write the answers you hear from Him. He had the Bible written for us. It is His letters to us. He appreciates when you write to Him. Express your thanks, your thoughts and your feelings. Express yourself through your gifts and talents. Love the Lord your God in all that you do. Be free to return to Him the joy that He has placed in you through worship, song, dance, art, banners and flags. Play an instrument. Worship Him with the work of your hands, by doing it as unto the Lord with your whole heart.

God does not dwell in temples made of stones, but abides in us the living stones. Our bodies are the temples of the Holy Spirit. He inhabits the praises of His people. As we open our hearts to Him and give Him praise in our lives, we will experience His Presence in numerous ways. When we acknowledge Him, He will direct us in all areas of our lives.

Do you not know that you are a temple of God and that the Spirit of God dwells in you? (1 Corinthians 3:16)

We are His Abode.

Dear Jesus,

I want to meet you in person. I answer the call, open my heart and ask you to come in. You are welcome in this place. Come abide in me. Fill me with your love. Fill me with your Holy Spirit. I ask you for that encounter that will empower me to become one with you and more like you. Thank you for forgiving me of all my sin and bringing me into your family.

Your New Child!

"The Kingdom of God is within you." (Luke 17:21, NKJV)

Remember wherever you go, He is with you.

ABIDE

I will sing of Your goodness
I will sing of Your mercy
I will sing praises to You
O Holy King
You are great
You are great
Signs and wonders
Follow Your Name
You are great
You are great
You remain
Forever the same
You touch our hearts
And turn them to You,
That we never stay the same;
But are growing more and more like You
Oh how great
Is our Eternal King
The One and the Only
Who brings us into sync
Abide, Abide
Forever in My Love
Abide in Me
Your Heavenly Maker from above.
Open the floodgates
Of your hearts
Let the Love of God flow

Let His Love flow
Open the doors
Let Him in
He wants to
Make you new again
Abide in Him.

JUXTAPOSITION

Drawing nearer
Ever nearer
To my Saviour within
Leaning on the Lord
My Maker and Creator
The One who loves me more
Who beckoned me through the door
To safety
To intimacy with Him
Come in, come in
Come and know Me more
Learn My ways and thoughts
I have great plans
You are a gem in my crown
I have sought you
When others have let you down
I am your Creator
The giver of peace
Lean on Me, seek Me
You will find Me
I will bless you with health
And length of days

Trouble and turmoil, they are near

But don't fear
I am here
Peace to you – to your thoughts
Come closer now my dear
I'll hold you close
Nothing will get near

There is Hope in times of trouble
Blessing and peace are yours
Let go of all fears
I am The One who hears
I hear your prayers,
Your thoughts
Your beliefs, your regrets, your reliefs
Yes, I know all things about you
I am near.
Juxtaposed, as close as One can get.
Only I can get that close.

Cloven Tongues of Fire - Acts 2:2-4

CHAPTER 6

HIS HOLY SPIRIT

The Advocate, Our Helper

> *"By this we come to know (perceive, recognize, and under-
> stand) that we abide (live and remain) in Him and He
> in us: because He has given (imparted) to us of His
> [Holy] Spirit."* (1 John 4:13, AMPC)

He is the one who points us in the right direction, toward Jesus.
He is the Spirit of Truth, who leads us into all truth, by nudging
us left or right, wait or go to keep us on the path following Jesus.
He directs our paths.

There was a time in my walk with God where I felt things chang-
ing. I had been going to church and trying to live right, but this
was different. The Holy Spirit was drawing me. I had bought a
copy of the Amplified Bible. It was like a fresh look at the Bible.
I found myself reading the references about the Holy Spirit and
highlighting various verses as I read. I had never seen or heard
people praying in tongues. I remembered that at the back of one
of my books, in the salvation prayer, it also asked for the Baptism
of the Holy Spirit. I went and found one of those books and
said the prayer out loud, asking God for the gift of speaking in
tongues. I started to speak by faith the sounds that formed. The

more I did this, the more it grew easier. Now that I was praying in tongues, I understood the Bible better. It seemed more alive. It wasn't just another book. This is where my relationship changed from knowing about God to knowing Him. He became more real to me. As I prayed in tongues, I was praying for the things that my own mind didn't know how to pray for. I started to change from the inside. I was activating the gifts of the Spirit and building up my faith. I became more aware of the voice of the Shepherd leading me.

One day, I made something of a supernatural discovery. My attention had been drawn to the books on my bookshelf. I noticed a book, pulled it out and looked at it, not even sure where this book came from. I sensed that this was a message for me and for right then. It was a blue-covered book by Madame Guyon: *Experiencing the Depths of Jesus Christ*. I came to know the Lord in a different way that day, waiting on Him and being quiet, listening on the inside.

I started to have more encounters in which I experienced the Presence and Love of God. Communication opened up with Him in a greater way. I started to have dreams. As I sought the understanding of these dreams, they grew. During the times I would sit quietly in His Presence or worshipping, He would give me poetry and pictures. I began to journal what I was hearing and seeing. Sometimes the journaling would simply be writing "Thank You!" over and over again, or expressing His Name and greatness.

The more that you seek Him, the more you will find Him.

In one of the times of worshiping and waiting on the Lord's Presence, I began pondering on the Holy Spirit. We call God, the "Father" or "Abba." We call the Son, "Jesus" or "Yeshua." I felt as if there should be a more personal name to call the Holy Spirit, as well. I asked what His name was or what name to call Him.

I heard the word: transcendent. Then the writing of this poem flowed.

TRANSCENDENT

Transcendent Beauty

Heaven Sent

Transcendent, our heaven-sent representative
of the Presence of our Heavenly Father.
He sent us His very essence to dwell within us,
To woo us into a deeper knowing of Him
The very Presence of Love Himself comes into every fibre of our being,
Into the recesses of our soul, making us whole.
As we invite Him in
As we seek Him
Look for Him
Sit in quiet, waiting for Him
Explore and know Him more.
The mystery to be unveiled
Look into The Book and find Him there
As He whispers in your ear, with the still, small voice;
"Come, follow Me."
He will show you the way
He calls you at every turn
Lifts you when you fall
Encourages you to keep going
"This way. This way."
Imitate Me
See, this is how you do it
Be like Me
Love like Me

Forgive like Me

Oh worship Him
Love and adore Him
Honour and revere Him
Fear, reverence and respect
As you give Him your whole heart
He will fill it to overflowing with His Love
Liquid love
Rivers of Living Water
Give Him your hurts, fears, regrets, pain from the past
Empty your heart so that He can make it full
He came to heal the broken-hearted
Whatever has broken your heart,
Tell Him
Let it go
Forgive
Release
This makes room to hold His gold
He purchased you with a price
Doesn't matter whether you have been naughty or nice
For all have fallen
Ask Him inside
Then there will no longer be any need to hide
By His blood you have been bought
By His blood be washed
Now you'll glow
Good as gold
No more fear or shame
Be bold
Be baptized by water
Be baptized by power
Let love enter in.

"Transcendent." Our thoughts cannot really grasp the fullness of who He is; it is beyond our comprehension. He is not seen and yet I know He exists. He came from heaven to earth. The Holy Spirit transcends the universe or material existence. Now that the Holy Spirit resides in me, my experiences are no longer only realized through my natural senses, but beyond those limits, making them transcendent. I think the word "transcendent" describes the Holy Spirit who was with God at the beginning of creation, hovering over the waters and is here with me now.

Jesus said that it was good for Him to go away so that he could send the Helper. In 1 Corinthians 12:1 it says; "Now concerning spiritual gifts, brethren I do not want you to be ignorant;" and in verse 14:1 it says to "pursue love and desire spiritual gifts." 1 Corinthians 12:31 tells us to "earnestly desire the best gifts." In Luke 11, we are encouraged to ask for these gifts.

We need the power of the Holy Spirit to teach us and lead us in the right way: His way. He has a much better way for us to live than by our own way. He knows what is ahead. It is like when I would lead my horse; I would know where I was leading her to and she would have to trust me in where I was taking her. He says that we are to follow him. It is by the prompting of the Holy Spirit that we are directed or led in the right direction, that sense we have on the inside of being right or wrong. That feeling you get on the inside of peace or no peace, ease or uneasiness. There have been times where I have felt compelled to do something and didn't follow through on it and wished I had. That is the voice of the Holy Spirit, the inner witness.

When we pray in tongues, we are building up our faith and praying out the mysteries, the things that we do not yet know. This became a reality for me one day. I had woken during the night and was feeling uneasy. Praying in tongues was new to me. I felt the compulsion to get up and begin praying in tongues. I prayed for quite some time. When the uneasiness had left, I went back to bed. In the morning someone called to tell me to turn on the TV and told me of the 9/11 attack. Was that what I was praying for? I was in awe of what God had me do. A few years later, I had a similar experience. I was prompted to give a friend a call and pray in tongues together. As we did, I heard the name of someone specific to pray for. On the inside, I heard "Step back, step back". I said these words out loud. The next day, I was informed that this person whose name I heard was a couple of steps away from being hit by a car and had narrowly escaped from death.

> *"In the same way the Spirit also helps our weakness; for we do not know how to pray as we should, but the Spirit Himself intercedes for us with groanings too deep for words; and He who searches the hearts knows what the mind of the Spirit is, because He intercedes for the saints according to the will of God.*
>
> *"And we know that God causes all things to work together for good to those who love God, to those who are called according to His purpose."* (Romans 8:26-28)

Romans 8:28: "And we know that God causes all things to work together for good to those who love God, to those who are called according to *His purpose.*" is often quoted to give reason for a situation or circumstance, but in context, it is the Holy Spirit and praying in tongues that is being spoken of here. When we pray in tongues "all things" will be worked out.

We also worship and give praise to God, by praying and praising in the language given to us through the Holy Spirit. When I sing in this heavenly language there is a great joy that comes inside me. John 11:33 says, "Jesus groaned in the Spirit" and Luke 10:21 says, "He rejoiced greatly in the Holy Spirit". In Ephesians 5:18 and 19, we are encouraged to be filled with the Spirit and speak and sing to ourselves.

"Wherefore be ye not unwise, but understanding what the will of the Lord is. And be not drunk with wine, wherein is excess; but be filled with the Spirit; Speaking to yourselves in psalms and hymns and spiritual songs, singing and making melody in your heart to the Lord."
(Ephesians 5:17-19, KJV)

Through the Holy Spirit, I received the gift of poetry. This was not a natural talent that I previously had. It came from setting aside time to worship God. I guess you could call it a love language. When I pray in tongues, I will hear words in English and as I write more words flow. At the end of the poem *Transcendent*, it says; "Be baptized with water, be baptized with power". Both of these baptisms brought different changes. As my relationship with the Holy Spirit grew, I felt a strong desire to be baptized. Previously, I had been baptized by sprinkling of water. Now I desired to be immersed. When I followed through on this, and received a full immersion baptism, I felt a difference. It was like a rebirth. Yet, it was through the baptism of the Holy Spirit that I was experiencing inner change and growth, His power to change. I am enjoying my encounters with the Holy Spirit. You will, too.

WITH HIM

Wisdom, power and might
Through the Holy Spirit we are given insight
There are truths to be revealed
Ways made straight
And deals to be sealed
Everything in His time
Have an openness to different ways of doing things
Eyes to see much further down the road
Wonders and miracles to behold

Dare to dream,
Even greater things
The light of His truth will make the way clear
Open your ears and hear
Reside in His Presence
Abide in His Love
Draw near

Father,

I ask for the good gift of the baptism of the Holy Spirit, with the evidence of praying in tongues. Fill me with the power of the Holy Spirit and equip me to see and hear spiritual things.

Thank You!

Now, by faith speak out the words He gives to you.

CHAPTER 7

COMMUNION

Come into Union with Him

Communion:

The sharing or exchanging of intimate thoughts and feelings, especially when the exchange is on a mental or spiritual level.
The service of Christian worship at which bread and wine are consecrated and shared.
(Definition from Canadian Intermediate Dictionary 1979 edition)

Communication refers to the many different ways we express ourselves to God and hear from Him, including prayer. We discuss with Him the things we need help with, making our requests and giving Him thanks for the answers. At times waiting quietly, just spending time with Him by thinking about Him and His name or waiting to hear an answer or instruction. This may include fasting, through which we submit our wills and plans to His and not to the earthly desires. At other times, we may pray in tongues until we hear from Him. When He gives us a specific scripture, we declare it as if it already is, or proclaim it. Speak life and blessing to situations, then turn all our concerns and requests over to the Father, thanking Him that it is done. Believe and act as if it is already accomplished. This is faith. Faith speaks life and calls into existence those things that are not as though they already are. Give him all your cares. He cares for you.

Union:

An act or instance of uniting or joining two or more things into one
A uniting in marriage
The growing together of severed parts
A unified condition
Something that is made one; something formed by a combining or coalition of parts or members
(Definition from www.merriam-webster.com)

"Becoming like one." This is what Paul says about the mystery of Christ and the Church. We are to become one, which can be likened to a marriage. Two becoming one and living in harmony, our thoughts becoming like His, by spending times of intimacy with Him and honouring and revering Him.

Marriage Like Christ and the Church

> "*Wives, be subject to your own husbands, as to the Lord. For the husband is the head of the wife, as Christ also is the head of the church, He Himself being the Savior of the body. But as the church is subject to Christ, so also the wives ought to be to their husbands in everything.*

> "*Husbands, love your wives, just as Christ also loved the church and gave Himself up for her, so that He might sanctify her, having cleansed her by the washing of water with the word, that He might present to Himself the church in all her glory, having no spot or wrinkle or any such thing; but that she would be holy and blameless. So husbands ought also to love their own wives as their own bodies. He who loves his own wife loves himself; for no one ever hated his own flesh, but nourishes and*

cherishes it, just as Christ also does the church, because we are members of His body. For this reason a man shall leave his father and mother and shall be joined to his wife, and the two shall become one flesh. This mystery is great; but I am speaking with reference to Christ and the church. Nevertheless, each individual among you also is to love his own wife even as himself, and the wife must see to it that she respects her husband." (Ephesians 5:22-33)

COMMUNION

The Lord's Supper - Passover

Do this in remembrance of Me.

> *"And when He had taken a cup and given thanks, He said, 'Take this and share it among yourselves; for I say to you, I will not drink of the fruit of the vine from now on until the kingdom of God comes.' And when He had taken some bread and given thanks, He broke it and gave it to them, saying, 'This is My body which is given for you; do this in remembrance of Me.' And in the same way He took the cup after they had eaten, saying, 'This cup which is poured out for you is the new covenant in My blood.'"* (Luke 22:17-20)

The first poem I wrote, called Communion is about the Lord's Supper.

He did this for you.

COMMUNION

The Body broke,
to make me whole.

The Blood,
to wash me white as snow.

"Truly, truly, I say to you, he who believes has eternal life. I am the bread of life.

He who eats My flesh and drinks My blood has eternal life, and I will raise him up on the last day. For My flesh is true food, and My blood is true drink. He who eats My flesh and drinks My blood abides in Me, and I in him. As the living Father sent Me, and I live because of the Father, so he who eats Me, he also will live because of Me. This is the bread which came down out of heaven; not as the fathers ate and died; he who eats this bread will live forever." (John 6:47-48 and 54-58)

"Jesus said to them, 'I am the bread of life; he who comes to Me will not hunger, and he who believes in Me will never thirst.'" (John 6:35)

"And he took the seven loaves and the fish, and giving thanks, He broke them, and started giving them to the disciples, and the disciples gave them to the people." (Matthew 15:36)

This is *Hamotzi*, the Hebrew Blessing for the bread. I think this is the "thanks" that Jesus gave when He broke the loaves and fish.

בָּרוּךְ אַתָּה יְיָ אֱלֹהֵינוּ מֶלֶךְ הָעוֹלָם

Barukh atah Adonai Elohaynu melekh ha-olam
Blessed are You, Lord, our God, King of the Universe

הַמּוֹצִיא לֶחֶם מִן הָאָרֶץ (אָמֵן)

ha-motzi lechem min ha-aretz. (Amein)
who brings forth bread from the earth. (Amen)

There is life and strength imparted to us in remembering Him and taking communion.

HEALING BREAD OF LIFE

Healing is the children's bread.

Jesus is the bread of Life.

He is your healer,

your Redeemer,

The everlasting Prince of Peace,

your Eternity.

Eat of Him,

Drink of Him,

Be washed, be cleansed, be made whole.

Be transformed by the renewing of your mind with the washing of the Word of God.

You can do all things through Him.

FORGET the former things

BEHOLD the new thing!

He is doing a new work in you and through you.

Put off the old man and put on the new man.

You are a new creature in Christ Jesus!!!

The old is past.

TODAY is a NEW DAY!

All things have become new!

Commune with Him.

CHAPTER 8

THE BRIDEGROOM IS COMING

THE BRIDEGROOM IS COMING

O Lord, my heart's desire is for you.
There is a longing, a wanting, that is so great
More than my heart can contain.
It feels as though my heart will burst in my chest.
It is calling for you to come near.
The Bridegroom is coming.
He is coming.

It is in the dark of night, near the break of dawn.
The New Day is nearly here.
He is coming.
The Bridegroom is coming.

My Body is restless and can't sleep.
It longs for Me
The Prince of Peace
The Lover of your soul
You long for that eternal love,
The One who will not let you down.
The One who calms your soul,
Tells you of your great worth.
"You are valued,
You are prized."
It is you that I have eyes for.
Yes, there is a call in your heart for Me.
Seek Me
Seek Me early and you will find Me.
The foolish cast off the draw of My Spirit on their hearts.
They are not ready.
They sleep.
They slumber.
They ignore My call.

I am calling all, not just the few.
But they have refused My courting.
Instead they look to the world and the desire of the flesh.
I have warned them to put away all uncleanness,
Lust of the flesh, fornication, perverseness;
But they do not listen.
They have been warned that the time is short;
But will not listen.
Again, I say, "Take heed."

Lord I come down that dark path in the night,
To meet You, my Light.
The call of my heart is so strong.
It can't be long,
'Til I meet with You.
O the longing of my heart
How can I contain it?
It is much greater than mere mortal life.
And yet Lord, you chose to live in this vessel.
You fill me with fresh oil.
My heart burns for you
And shines forth Your Light,
That penetrates the darkness
Bringing hope and direction to the lost.
You are my campfire,
Who draws me close, gives me comfort and warmth.
My gaze drawn into the middle of the blaze,
Captivated by Your movement, Your strength
And the light of Your glory.
O Lord, You are Holy!
There is no truer, purer love than Yours.
You are welcoming, inviting,
O so exciting.
Touch my heart with your fire,

That I may burn with the same intensity.
I can't express the depth of that longing.
You are great
You are magnificent
Jesus, Yeshua
King of Kings
Lord of Lords

To those that sleep and slumber,
I say, "Arise, arise."
He is risen
He is on His way here.
The Bridegroom comes
Make yourselves ready
Prepare your hearts
Cleanse yourselves
Put on His garment of righteousness.
His robe is honourable
No more shame
No more sorrow
No more regret
He not only cures your heart,
He makes it whole
Be holy for He is Holy

Cast off those heavy garments of remorse, sin and shame.
Don't pick them up again.
Be covered in My Love,
My Blood,
Jesus

CHAPTER 9

THE INVITATION

THE INVITATION

The Lord says,
"Come away with me, my bride.
Enter into my shelter and abide.
Come unite with me and become one.
In this place of unity you will hear My voice.
Keep close.
Listen.
I will whisper softly to you.
Hear how much you are loved.
There is a purpose and a plan for you.
Keep close to me, to hear each step to take."

The King sends an invitation to come to the wedding of His Son.

> "The kingdom of heaven is like a certain king who arranged a marriage for his son, and sent out servants to call those who were invited to the wedding." (Mathew 22:2, 3)

Come to the Wedding Feast!

The KING

Invites you to come to the marriage supper of

The LAMB

Listen!
I stand at the door and knock;
if any hear my voice and open the door,
I will come into their house and eat with them,
and they will eat with me. Rev 3:20

LOCATION: The Royal City

REFRESHING: The Holy Spirit will be poured out on all who call and you will be filled with Living Water

RSVP: I confess with my mouth, Jesus as Lord and believe in my heart that he came in the flesh as the son of God and was raised from the dead.

Happy are those who have been invited to
the wedding feast of the Lamb.

"Then a voice came from the throne, saying:

'Praise our God,
    all you his servants,
you who fear him,
    both great and small!'

Then I heard what sounded like a great
multitude, like the roar of rushing waters and
like loud peals of thunder, shouting:

'Hallelujah!
    For our Lord God Almighty reigns.
Let us rejoice and be glad
    and give him glory!

For the wedding of the Lamb has come,
    and his bride has made herself ready.
Fine linen, bright and clean,
    was given her to wear.'

Then the angel said to me, 'Write this: Blessed are those
who are invited to the wedding supper of the Lamb!' And
he added, 'These are the true words of God.'

"I saw heaven standing open and there before me
was a white horse, whose rider is called Faithful and
True. With justice he judges and wages war. His eyes are
like blazing fire, and on his head are many crowns. He
has a name written on him that no one knows but he
himself. He is dressed in a robe dipped in blood, and
his name is the Word of God." (Revelation 19:5-9,
11-13, NIV)

"The river of God is full of water." Psalm 65:9 NKJV

The time is short!
Come to the Wedding Feast.

Parable of the Marriage Feast (Matthew 22:1-10)

> *"Jesus spoke to them again in parables, saying, 'The kingdom of heaven may be compared to a king who gave a wedding feast for his son.' And he sent out his slaves to call those who had been invited to the wedding feast, and they were unwilling to come. Again he sent out other slaves saying, 'Tell those who have been invited, "Behold, I have prepared my dinner; my oxen and my fattened livestock are all butchered and everything is ready; come to the wedding feast."' But they paid no attention and went their way, one to his own farm, another to his business, and the rest seized his slaves and mistreated them and killed them. But the king was enraged, and he sent his armies and destroyed those murderers and set their city on fire. Then he said to his slaves, 'The wedding is*

ready, but those who were invited were not worthy. Go therefore to the main highways, and as many as you find there, invite to the wedding feast.' Those slaves went out into the streets and gathered together all they found, both evil and good; and the wedding hall was filled with dinner guests."

Dear Treasures in Earthen Vessels,

You may have felt forgotten or of no use or value, but I have a great purpose for you. Though you may not glimmer and shine at this moment, you have such a large capacity to receive and believe. As you become whole, you will pour out the sweetest wine available throughout all time, for the groom has reserved the best for last.

I am here to unearth the hidden treasures, saved for such a time as this. Welcome! Enter in. Find rest for all of you who are weary and heavy-hearted. I have come to heal the broken-hearted.

Come and dine with me,

The Bread of Life

The Living Water

The Door is Open!
Enter in.

CHAPTER 10

THE RESPONSE

An invitation requires a response.

How will you respond?

Will you open the door?

Will you say, "Yes"?

Will you call upon The Name?

Will you choose Life?

COME!

Come to the wedding feast of the Lamb.

Father,

I accept your invitation.

Thank you for the invitation to come and eat with you. Thank you for Your Word. Jesus, I call on Your Name to become one with you. Today I choose to follow you, the Good Shepherd!

Thank you!

"Enter His gates with thanksgiving

And His courts with praise.

Give thanks to Him, bless His name." (Psalm 100:4, NASB)

"Enter with the password: 'Thank you!' Make yourselves at home, talking praise. Thank Him. Worship him." (Psalm 100:4, MSG)

AMAZED AT YOUR LOVE FOR ME

Amazed, amazed
I am truly amazed
Your eyes are lit with fire
You fill my heart's desire
You love me with burning love
You set my heart on fire

You draw
My every breath
I am truly alive,
With the love I feel inside
You are my all in all
My heart's very beat of life.

You open my eyes,
Cause me to see
Your love for me.
It is so great!

O Lord my God,
Lord my God

My all in all
I submit
To Your call.

Amazed, amazed
I am truly amazed
At Your love for me
On the cross You set me free

Amazed, amazed
Your love sets me free

Yes, I am truly amazed at how much the Father loves me! A day when I really needed encouragement, He presented me with roses. As I was out for a walk, I felt directed by the Holy Spirit to go a certain direction. I came upon a very pleasant surprise. Nestled up close to an apartment building on a cold January day, there was a rosebush in full bloom. Thank you, Abba, for the roses!

A *PRAYER OF DEDICATION*

Talk to God, the Father, the Son and the Holy Spirit.

Father God,

I come to You in the name of Jesus. I know there are times I have messed up, blamed myself, blamed others, not forgiven, but no matter what it is, I believe that Jesus came and paid the price to set me free. I choose to forgive others that I also may be forgiven. I choose to forgive myself. I release all hurts and blame. I ask for and receive Your gift of salvation. Jesus, I answer Your call. Come in through the door to my heart. Fill me with Your Holy Spirit. I ask for the baptism of the Holy Spirit with the gift of praying in tongues, that I will pray the mysteries that I do not know how to pray with my own understanding. I thank You for all that you have done for me. I ask You to direct my steps and cause my thoughts to line up with Your thoughts and plans.

Thank you!

A PRAYER TO CONFESS

(Inspired by these scriptures: Philippians 1:11; Romans 8:10; Romans 5:17, 2; Corinthians 5:17; Colossians 1:11; and 1 Corinthians 1:30)

Jesus Christ lives in me; therefore, I am a new creation.
The old moral and spiritual condition has passed away.
The fresh and the new has come.
I have His Righteousness in me.
I am strengthened with His Power to do things His Way.
(You may want to write this on a card and carry it with you. Say this out loud daily and see the change in your life.)

CHAPTER II

MY PSALMS

"I am the Alpha and Omega,' says the Lord God, 'who is and who was and who is to come, the Almighty."'

"'Write in a book what you see and send it to the seven churches:'" (Revelation 1:8 and 11)

"My heart overflows with a good theme;

I address my verses to the King;

My tongue is the pen of the ready writer." (Psalm 45:1)

Here are some more poems and words that I received during worship:

LOVE LIVES THERE

Close your ears and listen with your heart
LOVE lives there
I live there
I will lead and guide you
Do not be distracted by the cares of this world

Draw from Me the grace and strength
You have captivated My heart
Listen deeply
Feel intently
Love resides there
Grace and compassion, love for the lost, hurt and dying

AN ENCOURAGING WORD!

Don't despair
Jesus is there
He'll take care
Whatever it costs
He'll provide
Our part is to abide
Abide in Him
He'll not chide
He will provide
Jesus is Lord
Lord above all
Above all troubles
Look up, Look up

May the Lord bless you,
and prosper you.
You are in His hand.
You are in His heart.
He will not depart.
You are His most cherished prize.
The apple of His eyes.
The Father loves you.

Be encouraged!

It is a new day
A new hour,
A day of His Power!
Be prepared,
To go about the Father's business.
He has many surprises in store
More than before
An increase in anointing,
Miracles you have hoped for,
Are through the open door.

His Love and Grace be upon you.

HERE I AM

For over the hills and far away
Your praise will ring throughout the day
You are the Mighty One
In whose hand we are held
Not to be removed
But held eternally
We delight in You
Your joy gives us strength

Deep within you,
There is a song in your heart
That will not depart
For I will never leave you
Nor forsake you
But give you joy everlasting
The strength to battle
The hands to war
The voice to roar

Christ has risen
The Daystar is here
His brightness shines
Causing you to rise

Where are your eyes?
Look up here,
My dear.
Come up here,
Where you belong
I'll hold you in My arms
You'll not be harmed
Come close,
Closer still
'Til you hear the innermost heartbeat of life
Life in the inner courts
Where you will dance with me
It will be so pleasant
You'll see
Come away with me

Love you Lord
Hold my hand
Take me to that
New and faraway land
Draw me closer
Closer still
My ear will hear
What You hear
What You have to whisper to me

Wait, wait and see
Deeper still

Come further out
The waters will not overtake you
Come through
Come through
I'll empower you

Press in
Press in
Here I am
Here I am

Where are you, O My Love
Come closer still

I'll open your eyes,
To see what I see,
And your ears to hear what I hear.

This is a New Day
A New Hour
A much greater hour
Greater are these days,
Than your earlier days

Receive, receive
Receive
Receive what I have for you
Receive
Receive
It is Yours!

AGAINST ALL ODDS

Against all odds
The odds were stacked against you
But you came out shining and clean
The price you were bought with
Purchased you, redeemed

Against all odds
You've run the race
Against all odds
You take your place

The odds are stacked against you
But this is no game of chance
The Champ of all champs has bought you
And placed you on His side
The Winning Side

You decide
What is your side
Life or death
Light or darkness

Choose life
His life
Everlasting life
Eternal life

Take the step
It's up to you
He'll see you through
Through trials and temptations

Against all odds
You'll overcome
Against all odds
It will be done

You are worth the price!

TIMES IN HIS PRESENCE

Times of breakout,
Times of encounters,
Times of renewal are in His Presence
There is breakthrough and power in your praises,
For the Lord inhabits the praises of His people.
Mine is a more excellent way,
A way more enduring.
Be strengthened in My Presence.
A pure heart will purge the flesh.
Impure thoughts will deaden the heart.
Draw your thoughts to Me, that all may see and know that I am God!
I am the Mighty God, the One and Only God.
Cast away the cares and heavy burdens.
Manifest My Presence in your lives. Be filled to overflowing.
What's in our hearts?
Love the Lord your God with all your heart, for
out of the abundance of the heart it flows.
Come away with Me O My bride.

THE SON

Isaiah 60:1: "Arise, shine…"

There are cracks to be filled

Hearts to be healed
Equipping the labourers for the field

Wake up, wake up!
The call is here
The hour is very near

Shake off the slumber
Shake off the dust
Put on trust

Why do they worry,
Of what they can or can't do
It is Me in them
That will see this through

Am I not Mighty?
Mightier than mere men
Give Me the Glory,
The worship, the praise
Let it be Me they raise,
In these days.
Then the Son will shine brightly
and people will see,
and give to Him all the glory.

PRESENTLY

There is no time like the present.

Presently the Lord is with you
and always he is there
Even in the times of despair

He is our everlasting God
Filled with truth, peace, love and faithfulness
His love endures where ours fails
Draw near to His heart
Fill your heart with His love
Pour it out into others
Fill the need in empty lives
Pour into them until they are filled
and brimming over
Beaming and gleaming and made new again

STEEP IN MY PRESENCE

Holy is His Name
The name above all names
He has come to give us life abundantly
From here to eternity
It flows in us
And through us
Bringing refreshing
To dry and thirsty souls
Yes, all who are thirsty
Come unto Me
And I will give you
Living Water
To satisfy
To refresh
To renew
Behold I make all things new!
Put off the old
Put on the new
Transform your minds
Entwine your hearts with Mine

Fill your thoughts with Me
Worship Me
Come away with Me
I will grant you the desires of your heart
Where there is no self-seeking in your ways
Make My Ways your ways
Plan to steep in My Presence
Be infused in My Living Water
Be washed and cleansed and made whole

NEW SONG

(Inspired by Psalm 40:3)

There is a new song in my mouth
There is a new song in my mouth
There is a new song in my mouth

Filled with the Holy Spirit
Filled with Truth

There is a new song in my mouth

To worship You,
In spirit and truth
There is a new song in my mouth
To worship You
To worship You

You are the One and Only,
The True and Living God
Creator of heaven and earth
You are the One and Only

And we worship You

We worship You!

COME NOW

Come now and bless the Lord
Lean close
Hear His still, small voice
As you draw near
You will hear
Open your heart
Feel His Presence
Feel the wealth of His Love
His existence within you
His Spirit resides on the inside
It overflows to those around you
Let the Love of Christ overflow
It knows no boundaries

Behold the open door
Come
Come and spend time with Me
Push aside the distractions and cares
Put your trust in Me
Pause, stop and listen

DESTINY IMAGE

I am created in His Image.
I reflect the Son.
I am a new creature in Christ Jesus.
I am a jewel in His crown.

I am chosen.
I am loved.
I am adopted into His family.
I am accepted.
I am a pearl of great price.
I am valued.

AS YOU LEAD ME

To You O Lord
I give my praise
It is You I am thinking of
You give me life and length of days
O my Father, in heaven above
I give You my love

My heart and thoughts are drawn to You
You have rescued me and pulled me out of the pit
You give me strength and have instilled hope in me

Greater things are yet to come
A more prosperous way has been laid out before me
And yet with my eye it cannot be seen
My trust in You deepens as You lead me,
Guide me and encourage me on this path
You are causing a strength and a boldness to rise up inside
There is a tenacity that says, "I will not quit."
I will not quit believing in you
It is God that I desire to follow
He has a more perfect way
Of whom shall I fear or dread
To God I give my awe instead

Yes, Lord you are worthy of much praise
Your value cannot be measured
Your greatness is beyond comprehension
You are the Mighty King of Glory
I trust in Thee

Yes, it alone is You that my soul longs to know more
I want to walk in Your path
The right way You have for me
The way of life and not death
I trust in You to carry me through

You give me strength
I give You praise
You are mighty
You are great

HOPE

Hope, the rope I hold tightly to
The three-stranded cord of the Lord
Faith, Hope and Love
Knowing You will never let me down
Believing for those things I do not see
Because I know You love me!

Believing and cleaving.

THE GIFT

Behold the gold,
From the ancient days of old
God has a great gift for you,

If you will let Him out of the box
Do display His glory
Not your own schemes and plans
Transform
Don't conform
Open your eyes to see
Open your ears to hear
Great mysteries He has for thee

THE MIGHTY KING

You are the Mighty King of Glory.
I trust in You.
You are precious and cause me to draw nearer to You.
Yes, it alone is You O Lord
That my soul longs to know more
I want to walk in your path
The right way that you have for me
The way of life and not death
I trust in You to carry me through
You give me strength as I give you praise
Yes Lord,
I praise You
You are mighty
You are desirable
My heart yearns for You
Longs for you
Oh how I want to know You.

UNFAILING LOVE

You are my love
My unfailing love
You draw me close
And hold me near
You wipe away my tears
And calm my fears
You give me grace
And strength for this race

O Lord my heart aches
I feel so alone
What is my hope
But You alone

ENTER INTO HIS ARMS

Come enter into the arms of Love
The Savior sent from above
He came
He died
He rose again
To take all your pain from inside
He is yours
Reside in Him
Let Love enter in
He came
He died
He rose again
That things would no longer be the same
He covers you with His Love
He is the Saviour that returned above

You are His
Bought with the price of Love
Love, Love, Love

I CHOOSE YOU

My God
My King
Lover of my soul
My Everything

I trust in You, Lord
I really do – I want to really trust You
I want to fully rely on You

Help me to put away selfishness, thoughtlessness,
Fear, doubt and unbelief
I choose faith
I choose love
I choose peace
I choose You, Lord
The Everlasting Way!

INNER ROOMS

It is You, my Lord
That I am longing for
It is You that I adore
O Lord, how I yearn for You
My heart longs for You
I want to know You more
I want to hear Your heartbeat
To feel Your breath on my cheek

To hear You whisper in my ear

Yes, Lord,
It is You I am longing for
I want to know You more
You are the open door
Who beckons me
Come
Come in through the open door
And get to know Me more

Personally I invite you
Into the King's chambers
The Inner Courts
The Inner Rooms
Rooms of intimacy, secrets and mystery

Yes, it is that relationship of growing closer,
Deeper and more aware of Me
The Lover of your soul
The One who makes you whole
Again I say, "Come"
Come unto Me all who are burdened
I will take away your troubles and tears
Yes, my dear, come here

DRAW ME

O Lord
How beautiful and wonderful You are
My thoughts are drawn to You
You lead me by Your Spirit,
Ever closer to You

As I gaze into the flames
I feel the warmth of Your embrace
You give me grace
And length of days
You give me strength,
Endurance to run the race
My heart overflows
I feel Your Peace,
Your Presence

vAs I look into the blaze
I feel Your Presence in this place
You draw me deeper,
Wanting to know Your thoughts
Your heart
Your ways
You cover me with Your grace
You draw me near,
Putting Your robe of righteousness over me
You have washed me
Cleansed me
Healed me

OUR GOD SAVES LIVES

From the depths of destruction
Darkness looms
Our God saves lives
Our God saves; Our God saves

He overcame death and the tomb
He was raised to make me new

Broken dreams can come true
Our God saves
Our God saves

He shed His Blood for me and you
Now we joyfully shout
And give Him Praise
Our God saves
We give Him praise
Our God saves
Our God saves

Our God saves lives
From death and despair
He is The One who cares
He loves you and set you free

Our God saves lives
Our God saves; Our God saves

I WANT TO KNOW YOU

The cry of my heart
Is for You
Come closer
Closer still
I want to know You
I want to know You
Touch my heart
Make me whole
Erase the pain
Wash it away
Take me by the hand

Lead me by Your ways
Lead me in this new day
The cry of my heart is for You
Yes, only for You
You are mighty and true

FEAR THE LORD

(Inspired by Psalm 25:14 and Proverbs 2:1-5)

Fear the Lord
Draw near to Him
Meditate on His Word
Let it become real and alive in your heart.

I will fear the Lord my God
I will walk in all His ways
And love Him all my days
I will serve the Lord my God
With all my heart and soul
I will meditate on Your Word
And keep Your Commandments

I will fear You
I will serve You
Awe and Revere You
Mighty God
I will fear You

ADONAI

Adonai
Lord
Alpha and Omega
The Beginning and
The End
Aleph and Tav
את
Abba
Our Father

CHAPTER 12

MY MEDITATIONS

I recite, meditate on the Word day and night; that I may observe and do according to all that is written in it. For then I shall make my way prosperous and I shall deal wisely and have good success. I am strong, vigorous and very courageous. I am not afraid, nor dismayed, for the Lord my God is with me wherever I go. (Joshua 1:8)

I trust God, who gives life to the dead and I call into existence that which does not exist. (Romans 4:17)

I gird myself with strength—spiritual, mental and physical fitness—for my God-given task. I open my mouth in skillful and godly wisdom and on my tongue is the law of kindness, giving counsel and instruction. I am capable, intelligent and virtuous. (Proverbs 31)

I bless the Lord. O my soul, do not forget all His benefits. He forgave me all my iniquities and healed me from all diseases. He redeemed my life from destruction. He beautifies, dignifies and crowns me with loving kindness and tender mercy. He satisfies my mouth with good so that my youth, renewed, is like the eagle's.

I bless the Lord. I reverently and worshipfully fear Him and His righteousness is to my children's children. (Psalm 103)

I receive Your Words and treasure Your commands within me. I incline my ear to wisdom and apply my heart to understanding. I cry out for discernment and understanding. I keep Your Words and write them on the tablet of my heart. (Proverbs 2:1 and 7:1-3)

HOPE AND TRUST

(Inspired by Lamentations 3:24; Romans 12:12, 1; Timothy 4:10; Proverbs 3:5; Hebrews 2:13; Isaiah 50:10; Psalm 37)

"I'm sticking with God."
I say it over and over again.
He's all I've got left.
I diligently seek Him.
I rejoice and exult in hope.
I'm steadfast and patient in suffering and
tribulation; constant in prayer.
May the God of my hope so fill me with all joy and
peace, as I trust in Him so that I may Overflow with
hope, by the Power of the Holy Spirit.
I fix my hope on the Living God.
I trust in the Lord with all my heart.
I do not lean on my own understanding.
In all my ways I acknowledge Him and He directs my paths.
I reverently fear and worship the Lord and turn entirely away from evil.
It shall be health to my nerves and sinews and
marrow and moistening to my bones.
I lean on, trust in and am confident in the Lord.
My trust and assured reliance and confident hope is fixed in Him.
I trust in the Name of the Lord.

I rely upon God.

I commit my way to the Lord.

He shall bring it to pass.

I rest in the Lord.

I wait patiently for Him.

I trust in the Lord and do good.

I delight myself in the Lord.

He is my strength.

He will help me and deliver me because I trust in Him.

My mouth speaks wisdom.

The law of my God is in my heart.

I meditate on His Word.

I seek the Lord with all my heart.

SEEK FIRST

I am created in Christ's image. I seek Him first, His kingdom and His righteousness. I believe that with God all things are possible. I have faith to call things as though they already are. I speak to my mind and body to agree with God's Word. I speak to my thoughts and plans to become agreeable with God's plan and purpose. I declare that I am healed, healthy, will live long and will be satisfied, for the Lord's Word is in my mouth to satisfy me at my personal stage in life. I have peace of mind. I have the mind of Christ Jesus. I seek God first and His ways. I ask the Holy Spirit, the Teacher to teach me His ways.

I encourage you to find the scripture verses that speak to you and your situation and declare them. Enjoy your journey.

CHAPTER 13

MAKE HASTE

MAKE HASTE

Make haste, make haste
He is coming soon
In all His glory and splendor

He is here, He is here
Draw near
Nearer to Him
He welcomes you in

You are His, you are His
You make Him glad
As you obey His Voice
The Angels rejoice

Praise Him, Praise Him
Praise His Holy Name
Ever exalted
Name above all names
For His glory and majesty

He overcame
Gave you the power to do the same

He loves you with an everlasting love
Sent down from Heaven above
The earth to reclaim
What He has created for us, His creation
To love Him in return
Step into His ways
Heavenly ways
Lord above all things
Our King
Jesus, The Christ
The Messiah
Anointed One

~~~את~~~
Stay in tune with the Lord;
He is coming soon!
~~~את~~~

ABOUT THE AUTHOR

Lynda Lee Kjartanson is a Canadian of Icelandic descent with a Christian heritage. Though born in a small town, she has the adventuresome spirit of her forefathers and seeks to experience more of the global community that we live in today, calling many "family" internationally. She now resides in Vancouver, where she has experienced more of other cultures and languages. Lynda particularly has a love for Israel. Through a vast background of work and life experiences, she feels that she can identify with many. She has a passion to pray and desires to see people healed. She has lent an ear and prayed with many and has served as a telephone prayer partner with the Miracle Channel. God has given her a gift of poetry, which she is sharing here to encourage others to develop their own special relationship of knowing God.

CPSIA information can be obtained
at www.ICGtesting.com
Printed in the USA
LVOW05s2322040617
536940LV00049B/1995/P